A Succeed in America™ Mini-Dictionary

Ameri$peak™

the most common words and phrases

you need to know

to communicate effectively

in American business

Nara Venditti, Ph.D.

www.SucceedinAmerica.com

Ameri$peak™

A mini-dictionary of the most common words and phrases you need to know to communicate effectively in American business

A Succeed in America™ Mini-Dictionary

ISBN 9-9777054-1-2

Published by Succeed in America, LLC
P.O. Box 4724
Danbury, CT 06813-4724, USA
(203) 791-1107
www.SucceedinAmerica.com

For future updates, visit the Succeed in America Web site:
www.SucceedinAmerica.com

A Succeed in America™ Series and logo as well as the title and trade address are the intellectual property of Succeed in America, LLC.

First Edition 2006
Printed in Canada

International Standard Book Number 9-9777054-1-2
Library of Congress Control Number 2005911313

Here is What Business Leaders are Saying about this Book

"We do business in over 120 countries. And, as a leader with global responsibilities, it is critical that I communicate effectively wherever I am on the globe. Having a dictionary in English of the most common words and phrases used in American Business would be a great tool that can be provided to my global colleagues to help them better understand what I am saying... and to enable them to more effectively communicate with me!"

Thomas L. Schlick, Senior Vice President, Datacard Global Services, Datacard Group (The World's Leader in Secure ID and Card Personalization Solutions), USA

"Mastering business lingo is a *must*. This initiative is a very needed step towards better communication in our business. The use of a "communication" tool such as *"Ameri$peak"* could make our business-life a lot easier. For all those professionals, who are challenged to make the globe much smaller and more effective, I recommend to start reading [Ameri$peak] and practicing."

Pim Bonsel, Executive Vice President, Association for Service Management International, Executive Director, Research and Studies, Switzerland

"...the most common words and phrases you need to know ... is very valuable for foreigners, I think. It should surely expedite the learning of jargons and, at the same time, help them understand better the mentality of corporate America."

George N. Cardenas, Ph.D., Executive Vice President, Walsh Properties, American national, born in Spain

See more on the next page...

3

"I wish I had this [dictionary] several years ago, when I was trying to find my way in the business/professional world, where the use of idioms is so wide spread, there is hardly a sentence it is missing from. ...I'm sure this will be very handy to any one who is not too familiar with American English."

Eli Ben-Ezra, Senior Sales Engineer, NextNine Inc., Israeli national, USA

"It took me a year or two before I understood all of the nuances the American business jargon offers. This mini-dictionary will be very helpful for the person coming to US or a person dealing with a US businessmen in other parts of the world."

Mauri A. Korhonen, Vice President and General Manager, Ingenico Customer Services, US and Canada, Finnish national, USA

"This is a very interesting concept and I believe this will prove popular in many countries... I do have people working for me in the UK whose first language is not English. They would benefit from understanding and using these phrases. ...you [Nara Venditti] have created something unique that can add significant value to many people around the world."

Simon Morris, Director, Global Marketing, ClickSoftware (NasdaqSC: CKSW), UK

Read more on the back cover...

4

DEDICATION

To dynamic,
energetic, and expressive
American English

Acknowledgements

There is a number of people to whom I wish to express my sincere gratitude.

To begin with, I would like to thank my first English teacher, Rachel Zaretskaya, who cultivated my love for the English language as a child in the former USSR. I would also like to thank Prof. P. M. Alekseev for teaching me the principles of quantitative lexicology (a statistical method for developing dictionaries). I applied this knowledge when creating Ameri$peak. And a thank you to my Dad who encouraged me to develop and publish my first educational dictionary back in Moscow, Russia.

In addition, thanks to all of my fellow Americans who by using the colorful words and expressions in their daily communications have unintentionally provided the material for this dictionary. There are scores of individuals who participated in meetings, huddles, and negotiations, delivered keynote addresses, and wrote e-mails, trade magazines, newspapers, corporate press releases, memos, and modern American literature whom I would like to recognize.

A special thanks to my fellow Toastmasters and Cendant Mobility employees and leadership for creating expressive communication through the use of metaphors and idioms. I strongly believe that leaders can, and do inspire their employees by using these linguistic units in their speeches; and my own findings prove that the higher the position of an executive on the corporate ladder, the more frequent is their usage of idiomatic expressions. The trick is to reach all the members of one's audience!

Because we live in an age of globalization and rapid immigration there are scores of employees who speak English as a second language. The goal of this book is not only to help foreign born citizens to understand their American colleagues, but also to give them the tools to actively participate in discussions with their American counterparts.

Thank you, Robin DeMerrell, for contributing the final editing.

To my patient and knowledgeable editor Carey Reed, who is a talented and aspiring writer herself, my friend Cynthia Slater, who read the first draft of the mini-dictionary, and to Richard Hastings, Esq., Edina Soboleski and Phil Sarnik for reading segments of this book, and to Liz Abraham who conducted the first pass editing on a portion of the introduction, thank you very much.

Thank you, Russell Stockton for your cover design. I sincerely appreciate your patience, diligence and talent which greatly contributed to the appearance of my book!

And last and not least, to my family and friends who have provided me with support and encouragement throughout my life and career, thank you!

TABLE OF CONTENTS

Introduction

Those who know do not speak
Japanese proverb
A word is silver but silence is gold
Russian proverb

A man is as good as his word
American and English proverb

In the United States, verbal communication skills are crucial for establishing credibility and achieving success. Very often in the USA, the ability to express oneself and communicate with confidence will open more doors than a college degree and impressive credentials.

The Link between Vocabulary and Success in the USA

There is a strong correlation between a powerful vocabulary and a successful career.

Imagine conducting business in the USA, and an associate says to you, *"My plate is full 24/7, "* or *"Don't jump the gun on that product roll out."* What if you had an American

10

partner and during a meeting in your country heard the following series of expressions, *"we are stretched too thin"*, *"moot point"*, *"you guys are on a roll"* or *"back to Square One."* Or if you were new to this country, you came to work and heard your boss say, *"Hey, Ramon (Natasha, Edward, Akbar, Bjorn, Hao, Vasumathi, Sunil, or whatever your name is), tomorrow at the huddle we need to cover all the bases before getting the ball rolling on this project"*, and *"I don't want anything to fall through the cracks."* Finally, imagine someone sent you an e-mail, that said *"please submit your report on FAQ ASAP or by COB"* and concluded with *"FYI, TGIF, Regards, Stanley".[1]*

What you just read is American English and these are examples of words and expressions used frequently in American business. I collected a list of over one thousand of those most frequently used and then compiled those words and expressions into a mini-dictionary called Ameri$peak.™

The expressions mentioned above and many others come naturally to native Americans. This is in part what makes American English what it is: a flexible, dynamic, expressive language, full of metaphors, idioms, and acronyms. American English — especially as used in business — employs these types of words and expressions more frequently than any other language. Because of this, these features may, and do, cause confusion for non-native speakers. This confusion can slow down communication and negatively affect business interactions such as customer service, negotiations, training, day-to-day operations,

---

[1] The reader can look up definitions of these words and expressions in this dictionary.

employee performance, and overall efficiency in the workplace.

Who Ameri$peak™ is for and Why It Was Created

This mini-dictionary was created to help non-native American English speakers become more effective communicators in business situations and here is why.

Certain words and expressions occur in various business situations over and over again. And it is these types of words and phrases which one needs to learn first. Out of all the world languages (almost 4,000!) English is just about the richest in vocabulary. The Oxford English dictionary lists nearly 500,000 words and phrases while about the same number of technical terms remains un-cataloged. Do we need to use all of these words to be effective communicators? Luckily, we don't. The key is to know the *appropriate words* for the *right situations*.

Simply knowing more words will not help you to succeed. It is knowing the right words that will accelerate your success. You do not need to have an extensive vocabulary to be an effective communicator. To be an effective communicator you need to have the *correct vocabulary*.

Ameri$peak™ is for anyone who works or aspires to work in the USA and for those in other countries working with American colleagues. It is for native and non-native American English speakers who have been taught different versions of English acceptable in their respective countries.

The Most Common Words and Expressions

This glossary is a powerful tool for non-native American English speakers in business. Although relatively short, it is a comprehensive list of the most commonly used words and expressions in modern American business.

First, a note of caution: not all of these words and phrases are appropriate for every occasion, nor do they necessarily represent standard American English.

However, these are words and expressions you will hear frequently in the workplace, and you need to understand them.

Real-life contexts will help you judge how and when to use the words and phrases listed in Ameri$peak.

How Ameri$peak™ was Created

Throughout my many years of experience working in the USA as an educational programs developer for international executives, translator, interpreter and international relocation consultant, I have carefully analyzed real-life business communications. I have examined written and oral interactions in meetings, negotiations, keynote addresses, e-mails, trade magazines, newspapers, corporate press releases, memos, and modern American literature. By applying the principles of statistical lexicography, I extracted the most common words and phrases from those resources, and they are the words and expressions now contained in Ameri$peak.

About Ameri$peak Entries

1. Word Categories

Generally speaking, business communication vocabulary consists of three groups of words: units of general meaning, units essential to all businesses and units specific to individual professions. Ameri$peak entries fall under two categories: units of general meaning that occur frequently in business context, and words and expressions vital to all areas of business, from sales to research and development. Linguists often call this second category "core vocabulary."

2. Entry Formatting

a) The entries are in boldface type and to the left hand corner. The definitions and examples are to the right and are not bolded. Examples are italicized and given in brackets. Word entries commonly used in specific expressions substitute the word with ~ (a tilde) in the expression shown in brackets immediately following the entry and a colon. For instance,

Blow: (~ one's chance)   (to) fail at something; miss an opportunity

b) When one word or expression has two separate meanings, they are separated by a semicolon. For example,

Bottom line   dollar amount, profit, and money made; ultimate focus, final decision

c) When one word or expression has the same meaning as a previous entry, the previous entry is referenced using "See:" the entry in boldfaced type, in { }. For example,

Between two fires   {See: **Between a rock and a hard place**}

d) A group of entries starting with the same word are preceded by that word, not bolded and in capital letters. For instance,

HARD

Hard data   facts, numbers

Hard sell   aggressive selling; difficult to persuade

Hard to swallow   difficult to accept or believe, too much to handle

Hardball   aggressive approach

e) Abbreviations and Labels

(abbr) abbreviation (a shortened form of a word or phrase)

(acr) acronym (words made from the first letters of a series of words)

(adj) adjective

(ant) (a word with opposite meaning)

(inf) informal (informal usage, used informally)

(sl) slang (vernacular usage, lingo)

(smb.) somebody

(smth.) something

(syn) synonym (a word that has essentially the same meaning as the entry)

(to) a verb

(vulg) vulgarism (inappropriate words and expressions)

How Should You Use These Words and Expressions?

As stated earlier, although used in modern American business, not all of the words and phrases in this glossary are appropriate for every occasion. Especially avoid using units labeled as *slang (sl), informal (inf)* and *vulgar (vulg)*. However, you will hear this language often in the American workplace and understanding it is critical to clear communication. If you do not understand these expressions, you will feel "out of the loop" (left out, uninformed) and will miss out on many nuances of communication. Once you know these expressions and use them appropriately, you will "click" (connect, be accepted) faster with your American colleagues.

Ameri$peak updates at
www.SucceedinAmerica.com

As in most parts of the world, language in the US is constantly evolving. As trends and circumstances change, words and phrases are created which colorfully reflect prevailing sentiments. This is especially true regarding conversational language in the business environment. In order to keep up with the changes, we have created at www.SucceedinAmerica a link dedicated to frequent updates of words, expressions and concepts in step with an ever-evolving business environment.

We encourage you, the reader, to give us your input.

 This is the first edition and if you learned a new word or expression, found a mistake or misprint or have any comments, please e-mail us at nv@SucceedinAmerica.com.

Ameri$peak™

A

(a) **piece of cake**   very easy
[it is (a) piece of cake]

"A" team   the best team (from sports: "A" [best] team and "B" [next best] team)

Above and beyond
more than required (doing)

Above par   better than average, better than the usual

Abstract   summary of a paper or report

Ace in the hole   a secret weapon, somebody or something kept in reserve until the special time to bring them out, ensuring success (on a project, etc...)

Ace the ball   (to) do an excellent job

Achieve   (to) attain, reach, realize

Across the board
everywhere, including everyone and everything

Action   deed, step, motion

After the dust settles
the time after a period of chaos

Agenda   schedule to meet a goal; actions

Ahead of the curve
anticipating (business related) events

Ahead of the game   in an advantageous, winning position

Align (resources)
prepare, organize (resources)

Along those lines
something of the kind, similar

Ambiguous   puzzling, unclear, possible to interpret in two or more ways

Annual report   a yearly report that summarizes an

19

organization's financial performance and achievements

Approach   method, way of doing something

As it stands right now according to the present situation

ASAP   *(acr)* **as s**oon **as p**ossible

At the drop of a hat right away, immediately

At fault   responsible for an error, guilty

At the end of one's rope stressed out, at the limit of one's ability to cope with an adverse situation, the end

At the end of the day in the end, in the final analysis, finally, ultimately

Attack   (to) deal with something energetically and rigorously *[Attack the issues]*

B

Baby boomers US citizens born after World War II (time of a huge increase in the number of newborns)

BACK

Back end of this afterward, after the event is over

Back in the game back in action, once again in action

Back to Square One starting something from the beginning, starting all over again

Back to the drawing board {See: **Back to Square One**}

Back (smb. / smth.) up (to) support [Back me up on that!]

Backroom operations supporting units of business

Bail out (to) help out; leave a job, (syn) quit

BALL

Ball game an arrangement, matter, situation [That's a whole new ball game]

(the) **ball is in (smb.'s) court** it is now another's turn to do something

Ballpark approximate, rough [ballpark estimate]

Bark up the wrong tree (to) choose a wrong action or person, do the wrong thing

Bar none (without comparison) the best

Barebones insignificant, small, skimpy [Because the economy is up, employment packages are no longer barebones]

BE

Be a boon (to) be very helpful

Be behind (to) be reason for; overwhelmed with work, not up to speed (to) **Be behind the curve**   when major difficulties are in the past

Be better off   (to) be in a better position

Be deemed   (to) be considered as

Be driven by   (to) be motivated by, be powered by

Be in (someone's) face (to) be present when unwanted; annoying or pesky; confrontational

Be on a roll   (to) have momentum in getting to a goal

Be on the ball   (to) be aware, prepared

Be on to (smth.)   (to) know something critical that others don't

Be off   (to) leave; miscalculate

Be pushed back/ put off   (to) be delayed or postponed

Be underway   (to) start to function, develop

Be well on its way   (to) be making essential progress

Bear with (smb.)   (to) have patience with

Beat (smb.) to it   (to) do something before another person *[I was about to take care of this problem but you beat me to it]*

Beat (smb.) to the punch
{See: **Beat (smb.) to it**}

Beats me!   I don't know!

Beef up   *(inf)* (to) make stronger by adding manpower or equipment, reinforce by adding resources

Before one can say Jack Robinson suddenly, quickly

(to go) **belly up**   (to) fail (in business), go bankrupt

Benchmark   existing standards

Bend over backwards (to) do everything somebody else asks one to, do much more than required or necessary

Benefits   (usually non monetary) compensation for work (medical insurance, vacation days, etc.)

Beside the point irrelevant, not the focus

Best shot: (give it one's ~)
(to) do one's best *[I'll give it my best shot!]*

Between a rock and a hard place   between two obstacles; no-win situation

Between two fires
{See: **Between a rock and a hard place**}

Big   popular, *(syn)* huge

Big Blue   a nickname for IBM (International Business Machines)

Big deal!   This is not important!

Big fish   an important person or thing, *(syn)* big shot

Big gun   somebody with specific and exemplary

skills used to handle a specific situation

BITE

Bite the bullet   (to) endure a difficult situation, work through a difficult situation

Bite the dust   (to) be over

Bitter twist
unfavorable development

Black box   something unknown

Black hole   unknown entity *[it is going into a black hole]*

Blow: (~ one's chance)
(to) fail at something; miss an opportunity

Blow one's mind
fascinate, impress

Blow smoke   (to) lie; make a promise and not fulfill it; exaggerate

Blunt   (to) dilute, make less effective; speak directly

Blurb   standard piece of (normally written) information

23

Bog down (to) delay progress; slow to a stop

Boil down to (ultimately) result in

Boilerplate standard clauses or sections in a document

Book closings the finalization of annual accounting

Boom abundance; sudden development, increase

Boost (dramatic) increase

Bottom line dollar amount, profit, and money made; final decision, ultimate focus

Bottom out (*inf*) (to) hit the lowest point

Bounce (ideas) off (smb.) (to) get an opinion or advice, talk about (ideas)

Brainstorm (to) discuss; discussion with the purpose of resolving business issues

BREAK

Break down (to) divide into parts, subsections *[break down the business process]*; go out of order; fail, stop

Break off (to) fail, stop

Break out (to) separate into different groups

Break through (to) succeed after difficulties; success

Breakout (year) a record (year)

Bring up (to) mention something *[Bring up a perfect scenario]*

Broadband high-speed Internet access lines

Brutal intense, strong

Bubble up to (smb.) (to) check with somebody in a higher position

Budget financial plan; resources

Bugs mistakes, inefficiencies (usually in computer programs)

Bullet point (in a presentation)

Bump   (to) cancel (usually for a meeting with lower priority) and replace with another meeting *[Today's meeting was bumped to Monday]*

Buoy   (to) add support to, sustain

Burn one's bridges (to) permanently terminate relationships in a negative way, sever relationships with no opportunity of reconciliation

Burn-out   exhaustion and lack of motivation caused by work stresses

Bust (smb.'s) chops (*inf*)   (to) give a hard time, be difficult, to shock

Buy for a song   (to) purchase something very cheaply

Buy into   (to) accept, be persuaded

Buzzword   element of special lingo, term (frequently used in industry)

C

Call for (to) request; require

Call off (to) cancel

Call the shots (to) be in charge, determine the rules of the game, give orders

Camper a person *[He is not a happy camper]*

Can *(sl)* (to) dismiss, fire (from work), *(syn)* lay off

Can do attitude willingness to do seemingly difficult or impossible tasks

Canned *(sl)* standard, prepared beforehand *[a canned e-mail]*; dismissed (from work), fired, laid-off

Capture *(inf)* (to) document, record *[capture mistakes]*

Career hit (depending on context) career success or career damage

Cash in (to) exchange for the value in money, currency (originated from poker)

Catch on *(inf)* (to) understand

Catch 22 no-win situation (from a military rule, preventing anyone from avoiding combat missions)

Cautiously tread thin ice (to) proceed with caution

Cave in (to) weaken and to surrender

Caveat warning, caution; stipulation, limitation

CEO *(acr)* **c**hief **e**xecutive **o**fficer

CFO *(acr)* **c**hief **f**inancial **o**fficer

Change gears (to) change strategy, tactics; change topic of discussion

Cheat sheet
concentrated notes (main points for a speech or a presentation) used as a helping aid

CHECK

Check out (to)
consider, take a look at

Checklist/ list of to do's
a list of items and/or actions necessary to achieve a goal

Checks and balances
a series of rules designed to maintain a balance of power

Client base pool of steady, regular customers

Close a deal (to)
complete a business transaction

Close call almost; narrow escape

Close ranks (to) unite and fight together

Clout influence (over another person or within a group of people)

Clue into (to) update, provide important

additional information *[please clue me into the Client's issue]*

COB (*acr*) **c**lose **o**f **b**usiness (day) *[I will need this report by COB]*

C.O.D. (*acr*) **c**ash **o**n **d**elivery, paying for merchandise or a service upon delivery

Cold call sales call without an invitation or referral

(give the) **cold shoulder** *(inf)* (to) be unfriendly

Cold turkey abruptly, immediately *[He quit smoking cold turkey]*

COME

Come a long way (to)
make great progress

Come down to
(ultimately) result in, relate to *[it comes down to money]*

Come full circle (to)
change and develop; end up where one started through growth and development

Come into play (to) become a factor *[there are a lot of variables coming into play]*

Come off (to) appear *[he comes off as arrogant]*

Come on board (to) join (company)

Come out with (to) announce, launch (a new product)

Come up (to) become a subject of discussion

Come up (with) surface; offer

Come up the curve achieving the expected level of competency, learning, catching on to something

Come up to speed {See: **Come up the curve**}

Common ground: (reach ~) something in common, (to) agree

Complimentary free of charge

Consensus agreement, opinion shared by all

Conspicuously clearly, obviously, *(ant)* ambiguously, inconspicuously

Constructive criticism another's opinion given to help improve one's actions

Conundrum a challenge, mystery, puzzle, enigma

Cook the books to fudge, to misrepresent the company's accounting (generally to avoid taxes)

Cookie cutter generic; easy *[this is a cookie cutter project]*

Cool awesome, excellent, great, nice

Core main

Corporate culture the attitudes and customs of/ in a company regarding work values

Cover the bases (to) give or receive important facts about a subject or project, talk about important points, catch up on project issues

Crapshoot *(sl)* a gamble, a project/task with unpredictable results

Crush (to) eliminate, destroy

Cup of tea something you are good at or enjoy

Curve ball: (throw a ~) unexpected obstacle or event; unexpectedly change the parameters of your work or project, *(syn)* reshuffle the ducks

CUT

Cut a deal (to) make an arrangement

Cut back monetary decrease

Cut corners (to) achieve a goal without using a lot of resources (could be in a negative sense), take shortcuts, trim the process

Cut out (to) escape, leave early; fit, suited for *[(not) cut out for the job]*

Cut short (to) interrupt suddenly, stop abruptly

Cut (smb.) some slack *(inf)* (to) allow to do less than expected (favoritism); allow to perform without interference, not to influence, let somebody do the job his/her way

Cut to the chase (to) get to business, get to the point; be brief, stop talking; finalize *(syn)* wrap up, not beat around the bush

Cutting edge latest, modern, very recent *[cutting-edge technology]*

D

Data facts, figures, numbers, records

Day off a day on which one does not have to work *[I will take two days off next week]*

DEAL

Deal is off arrangement is canceled, arrangement did not go through

Deal with (to) manage, work with (usually with something unpleasant or negative) *[I will deal with this problem]*

Deliverable (projected) end result

Desktop a computer that sits on a desk

Devil's advocate a negative person, somebody who argues with another for the sake of discovering faults *[Stop playing devil's advocate]*

Differentiate (to) distinguish, make a distinction

Dig deeper (to) analyze in more detail, get to the details, look at something in greater detail

Dimension aspect

Diminutive very small

Ding *(inf/sl)* (to) criticize

Distill simplify, (syn) boil down

Ditto *(inf)* the same

Diversity range, variety; variety of cultures in the world and in the workplace

Do a double take (to) suddenly realize, understand something; look at something for the second time

Do one's homework (to) prepare, research before action

Do the trick (to) achieve desired results, solve the problem

Docket agenda *[let us put it on the docket, so that people start thinking about it]*

Dogma rigid beliefs, ideology

Double-back (to) retrace steps *[Can I double back with you?]*

Double check (to) check for errors carefully

Down and dirty (*adj*) preliminary, rough *[down and dirty proposal]*

Down to the wire nearing a deadline, running out of time; (to) almost be broke, almost be without money

Downside less desirable option or result

Downsize (to) reduce, reduce workforce, reduce in resource, lay off

Downsizing reduction of workforce

Drag on (to) make longer, prolong

Draw a line set conditions, set a limit

Drawback disadvantage

Drill down (to) get to further details

Drink from a fire hydrant (to) tackle a difficult task

DRIVE/DRIVEN

Drive (to) cause, make do something, necessitate, push, stimulate *[drive business growth]*

Drive someone up the wall (to) annoy someone greatly, make someone angry

Drive the bus (to) lead

Drive up (to) cause an increase in numbers or power

Driven focused, motivated *[project driven]*

Drop the ball (to) fail, lose an opportunity

Drum up (business) (to) attempt to increase sales, solicit (business)

Duck shuffler usually upper management, who will change one's

assignment or will ask for
a project to be redone just
as the project is being
finalized (derivative of
"put your ducks in a row")

Ducks in a row   in
good order *[you need to
have your ducks in a row
before the job interview]*

E

Ease (to) improve, make easier

Embrace (to) accept *[embrace the change]*

End of the rope the final result or end, when you can do no more, *(syn)* end of the line

End user client, customer, user of a product or service

End zone either of the marked areas behind a goal line

Evolve develop and change

Eye contact (to) look into the eyes of another (when speaking with them) *[to make ~ =to look directly at someone]*

F

FACE

Face (to) accept, confront

Face the music (to) accept, accept the consequences of one's actions, confront harsh reality

Face value the seeming worth or truth of somebody or something *[do not take things for face value]*

Fall behind lag

Fall for like or love; to be deceived *(syn)* to be duped

Fall into place (to) suddenly make sense

Fall short (to) fail to reach, not succeed

Fall through (to) not be done, happen

Fall through the cracks (to) get overlooked, to escape attention, to be forgotten

FAQ *(acr)* **f**requently **a**sked **q**uestions

Fast track accelerated promotion

Feedback advice, evaluation, opinion or response (in a business situation)

Fifty-fifty half to one side, half to another, equal(ly), even(ly)

Figure out (to) calculate, determine

Fill in to cover for an absent co-worker

Fill out (to) complete, fill in

Fire (to) dismiss from a job

Firewall a system barrier for undesirable messages or information (computer term)

Fishy suspicious, strange

(the) **fix** solution *[quick fix]*

FLOW

Flow chart a diagram showing steps of a business process

Flow into (to) move easily, naturally and quickly into

Fly by night unsteady, here today but not tomorrow (about a business or company)

Fly off the handle (to) become very angry and verbalize it

Focus (to) concentrate on

FOLLOW

Follow suit (to) follow somebody's example

Follow through (to) finish, finalize what was started

Follow up (to) make something more successful by checking on the status mid-process or after completion

For a song for a low price, very cheap

Framework structure, outline

Freaked out (to) stressed out, get anxious, *(syn)* have a break down

From scratch from nothing

Front end units of business dealing with customers and/or clients

Front room {See: **front end** }

Frontlines employees dealing with customers directly

F/U, f/u *(acr)* **f**ollow **u**p

Fuel (to) motivate, stimulate

Full-blown true; complete

Full-fledged {See: **full-blown**}

Fume (to) express oneself angrily

Funky off-beat, unconventional, unusual

FYI *(acr)* **f**or **y**our **i**nformation

G

Game plan intentions, plan, strategy

Gap what is missing, a hole, a missing part

Gap analysis determining what is needed, what it takes to get from A to B

Garden-variety everyday, ordinary, the usual

Gauge (to) estimate, assess *[...so that I could gauge what was done on this project]*

Generation X (Gen X) Americans born between 1965 and 1977

Generation Y (Gen Y) Americans born after 1978

GET

Get a grip on (to) take (firm) control over

Get a handle on (to) learn, understand

Get a piece (of the market) (to) get a share of the market

Get across (to) explain clearly

Get ahead (to) become successful

Get ahead of oneself (to) leave out important details while trying to deliver one's message

Get ahead of the game (to) get the advantage; work in advance

Get around to (to) find time for

Get away (to) leave for a short time

Get away with (to) avoid, escape doing the required amount of work

Get back in (to) reinvest in; return

Get behind: (~with work) (to) support; {See: **Be behind**}

Get carried away with (to) do too much of something

Get off easy (to) escape an unpleasant job or task

Get off the ground (to) get something started

Get on (smth.) (to) tackle, work on *[we will get on this right away]*

Get on a soapbox (to) lecture on a lost cause

Get one's arms around (smth.) (to) tackle a big task or project; difficult to handle, difficult to grasp a project (for one or a limited amount of people)

Get one's feet wet just getting started

Get slammed (to) be overburdened with work

Get the ax (to) be fired, get dismissed, get laid off, lose one's job

Get the ball rolling (to) get started, initiate action, start an activity

Get the hang of (smth.) (to) learn how to do something *[you'll get the hang of it eventually]*

Get the most out of (smth.) (to) take advantage (of a situation)

Get the show on the road {See: **Get the ball rolling**}

Get through (to) survive (a day, a week)

Get to the bottom of (smth.) (to) find out the real cause of something, find out who is responsible

Get to the point – get to the core of the matter without unnecessary introduction or details

Get under the skin of (to) understand fully; to bother

Get underway (to) get started and be in process

Get wind of (smth.) (to) learn about something (not intended for public knowledge)

Get your bearings (to) orient oneself, prepare

GIVE

Give a flavor (to) give an idea about something

Give (smb.) a hand (to) clap your hands for somebody; help

Give (smb.) a break to be easy on someone, not to be too demanding

Give (smb,) a hard time (to) be difficult

Give-and-take sharing; helping and getting help *[it's-a-give and take]*

Give back (to) repay, pay back

Give the cold shoulder *(inf)* (to) be unfriendly

Give it one's best shot {See: **Best shot**}

Give or take add or subtract, plus or minus

Give (smb.) the ball and let him/her run with it (to) trust somebody with a (project), turn over (a project) to somebody and let them make it a success on their own

Glass ceiling unofficial policy that prevents certain groups from being promoted (minorities, women, etc.)

Go after (to) try to get, obtain

Go back to (smb.) (to) check with somebody *[I have to go back to my manager on this offer]*

Go bonkers *(sl)* go crazy , *(syn)* go nuts

Go down the path (to) develop in a certain direction

Go Dutch when each person pays for themselves (in a restaurant)

Go for broke (to) risk everything at once, *(syn)* put everything at stake

Go full circle (to) go back to something; complete start to finish

Go-getter a person who is persistent, ambitious and works hard

Go over (questions) (to) explain, read or study again

Go the extra mile (to) make an extra effort

Go to bat for (smb.) (to) support somebody, help somebody out

Goal aspiration, objective, target

Going forward in the future; moving ahead

Golden shining, victorious, in good shape (on a project) *[You guys are golden]*

Grand slam perfect results, success

Grapple with (to) struggle with

Gray area ambiguity, something undefined

GROUND

Ground rule (usually unwritten) rules of what to do in a certain situation, guideline to follow

Ground work preparation (for a project)

Ground zero the bottom, the beginning – one can only go up from ground zero; zero, nothing

[many immigrants start at ground zero when they arrive in the US, becoming financially successful after some time]; the areas of 9/11 bombings in New York City

Groundbreaking extraordinary, pioneering

Growth opportunity chance to acquire new skills and be promoted at work

Gut feeling an inner-feeling, intuition

Gyrations *(sl)* efforts (often not yielding results)

H

Hammer out (to) discuss or debate, work out an agreement or project

HAND

Hand-holding dealing with a person requiring a lot of attention, a dependent person

Hand off to (smb.) (to) pass an initiative or responsibility to somebody else

Handout materials given out at a presentation, training or workshop

Hang on *(inf)* wait! ; (to) persevere , *(syn)* stick it out

Happen overnight (to) occur fast

HARD

Hard data facts, numbers

Hard sell aggressive selling, pushing the idea or product; difficult to persuade

Hard to swallow difficult to accept or believe, too much to handle

Hardball aggressive approach

Haul: (for the long ~) long term, a long time

Have a full plate /to have a lot on one's plate (to) be very busy with different projects, tasks

Have a long way to go far from the destination or goal

Have a shot at (smth.) (to) try something; get an opportunity for

Have an edge (to) have an advantage or superiority over competition

HEAD

Head for (to) move in the direction of

Head start an advanced or early beginning

Headhunter someone who searches for job candidates (usually with a salary in the range of $50,000)

Heads up: (to give [smb.] a/the heads up) advance warning, informing beforehand *[This email was sent to me from Mary, I thought I would forward it to you as a heads up]*; (to) warn

Here we go here it is

Hiatus break, interval, pause

Hidden agenda motives secretly advantageous to only one or a few

High and dry alone, with no help

High gear activity; top speed

Highflying acting in an extravagant way

Hit (to) damage *[my computer was hit by virus]*

Hit a grand slam (to) do an excellent job

Hit a speed bump (to) encounter an obstacle that slows progress

Hit a wall (to) encounter an obstacle that stops progress

Hit as a thunderbolt suddenly occurred, suddenly realized

Hit bottom (to) be at the very lowest (about prices)

Hit every bullet (to) cover every point in a presentation

Hit it off *(col)* (to) like each other

Hit or miss unplanned or uncontrolled

Hit the bottom all time low

Hit the bull's eye (to) go to the important part of the matter, reach the main idea, theme or topic

Hit the ceiling (to) get very angry

Hit the cover off the ball (to) do an excellent job, *(syn)* hit the ball out of the park

Hit the ground running (to) be able to perform a job or a task immediately

Hit the high spots (to) cover only the general and most important parts of a subject (during a presentation)

Hit the nail on the head
(to) speak or act in the most effective manner

HOLD

Hold on (to) wait (on the phone)

Hold on to (smth.)
(to) keep or save something; keep control

Hold out (to) keep secret

Hold up (to) delay

Hole defect, inefficiency *[there is a huge hole in the process]*

(a) **hole-in-one** (to) accomplish or succeed in doing something for the first time or from the first attempt

Homecoming triumphant and celebratory event

Homerun: (to hit a homerun) success; (to) win, succeed

HOT

Hot *(sl)* popular, important *[hot issue]*, *(syn)* in

Hot button(s) important issue, issue that may evoke emotional response, important needs of an individual, something which makes him/her tick

Hot issue important topic or subject

HR *(acr)* **h**uman **r**esources; **h**uman **r**esource professional

Hubbub noise, uproar *(syn)* racket

Huddle brief meeting to decide on a quick action

43

(usually without sitting down or going to a meeting room)

Huge *(sl)* important, fashionable *[that was huge]*

I

(An) **icon**   a powerful representation or symbol

In a heartbeat   in a second

In a nutshell   briefly and completely, in a few words

In line   conforming *[it is in line with company policy]*

In the long run   in the future

Incentive   enticement, inducement, motivation

Imperative   necessity, (*adj*) necessary, important

Increase   (to) add to, enhance, enlarge

Industry standard accepted in industry

Injection   quick addition

Ins and outs   every detail *[he knows the ins and outs of the business]*

Inside out   completely, throughout

Integration   addition; assimilation, mixing

Intrinsic (value)   its own value

Iron out   (to) solve or resolve problems or defects in a product or business process

(to be) **itching**   (to) be extremely eager to do something

It's a cinch   it is very easy

It is the name of the game!   This is the way things are!

J

Jam-packed very crowded

Joe (cup of Joe, box of Joe) coffee

Jostle (to) push others to reach a goal

JUMP

Jump down (smb.'s) throat (to) become very angry with someone

Jump ship (to) leave a company, quit a job (especially when the company is unstable)

Jump the gun (to) take action prematurely, be hasty, rush

Jump through a hoop *(inf)* (to) obey, do whatever you are told

Jump to conclusions (to) form hasty opinions about somebody or something without sufficient knowledge

K

KEEP

Keep (to) continue *[the same problems keep coming up]*

Keep an/one's eye on the ball (to) stay focused on the goals, not be distracted from the goal

Keep at (to) continue doing

Keep in line (to) keep under control

Keep in the loop (to) keep informed

Keep plugging (to) work hard

Keep score (to) maintain a count or record

Keep the ball rolling (to) continue the action or activity

Keep the momentum going (to) maintain the same level of energy and enthusiasm when doing a project

Keep track {See: **Keep score**}

Keep under one's hat (to) keep something a secret

Key players main participants

Kick back (to) not worry, relax

Kick-back gifts either monetary or non-monetary given illegally for favors in business

Kick in (to) start, come about *[economic recovery will kick in very soon]*

Kick in the balls *(vulg)* (to) shock

Kick it up a notch (to) start applying extra effort, *(syn)* take it up a notch

Kick off (to) start (with celebrations)

Kick to the balls *(vulg)* shock

Killer something negative, an obstacle

KISS *(acr)* **keep** it
simple sweetie

KNOCK

Knock (smth.) out
(to) finalize, finish quickly
[I will knock it out today]

**Knock (smb.'s) socks
off** (to) enthuse, excite,
impress

Kudos praise,
congratulations!

L

Laptop   a small portable computer

LAY

Lay the groundwork (to) do the initial preparation, get everything in place

Lay off   loss of job due to lack of work

Lay one's cards on the table   (to) deal openly and truthfully

Lay out   general agreement, plan

Lead dog   (project) leader

Learning curve   the period of time spent when becoming familiar with something, getting up to speed

Let it slide   disregard, pay no attention

Let the cat out of the bag   inform beforehand, let information out prematurely

Let's get the show on the road   let's get started, let us start

Leverage   advantage; (to) take advantage

Leveraged   having advantage

LINE

Line of business/work type of business/work

Line up   (to) organize, prepare, put together

Logistical   having to do with (business) processes and steps

Long range   far in the future

Long run   {See: **Long range**}

Long shot   with high risk, unlikely to succeed

Look at   (to) consider

Lose ground   (to) become worse, not improve, weaken

Lose one's shirt   (to)
lose a great deal of money,
lose everything

Lose track   (to) fail to
keep control or record;
forget

Lousy   (*col)* bad

Lump sum   money paid
all at once

M

MAKE

Make a call (to) contact by phone

Make a killing (to) make a lot of money

Make a point (to) emphasize, explain, *(syn)* call attention to

Make a splash (to) attract attention, be successful

Make hay when the sun shines (to) do something at the right time, not lose an opportunity

Make heads or tails of (smth.) (to) figure out, understand

Make headway (to) make progress

Make up (to) do what is lacking, *(syn)* catch up

Make waves (to) disturb, make one's opinion known

Make way for (smb.) (to) leave so that another can have control

Manage (to) administer, direct, run, supervise

Manager administrator, boss, supervisor

Mantra important word or expression *[Six Sigma is a corporate mantra]*

Map out (to) design (plan), outline, plan (a project)

Margin net sales minus the cost of goods and services, profit

Materialize (to) appear, occur

Max out (to) reach the maximum limit

Measure (to) assess, compute, determine

Measure up (to) be compatible, good enough, of a high enough standard

Meet someone half way (to) compromise

Meltdown (economic) failure

Memo written communication used internally in an organization

Metrics measurement results; methodology

Mindset attitude towards something, culture, philosophy

Miscues errors, mistakes

MISS

Miss the boat/bus (to) be too late for something important

Miss the point (to) not understand the essence of what is being communicated

Mission statement company's philosophy outlined briefly in one or a few sentences

MONEY

Money talks money influences people

Moot point further discussion or negotiation is useless

Move on (to) continue with your life without looking back, not dwell on past mistakes

Mull it over (to) think it over

N

NA *(acr)* Not Applicable

Nail down (to) make certain, make sure; understand; secure

Name of the game *(inf)* the crux, the heart of the matter; something that occurs under certain conditions

Navigation operating, routing, steering the system

Needy needing attention or help frequently (usually about a customer, often has a negative connotation)

Neck of the woods *(sl)* part of the country, city, state, town or region

Net (to) gain, acquire

Next to impossible almost impossible

Nifty clever, effective, ingenious

No-brainer *(inf)* something very easy, simple and very obvious

No frills no extras (about a product or service)

No-go not allowed to happen

No-show a person who unexpectedly does not attend a meeting, a person who did not attend a meeting

No sweat *(sl/inf)* easy; no problem

Not up to par worse than the accepted standard

O

Off-base   not agreeing with facts or reality

Off-beat
unconventional, unusual

Off-line   off the record; in private, without others around *[let's talk about that off-line]*

Off one's rocker   *(sl)* crazy, out of one's mind

Off-shore   non-US, foreign

Off-target   missing the point; not related to the goal

Off-the-cuff   speak or present without preparation, not prepared ahead of time, *(syn)* impromptu

Off-the-hook   with no further responsibility

Off-the-mark   not accurate, not standard

Off-the-record   (to) not be published or announced publicly

Off-the-shelf   not customized, standard (product or service)

Off-the-wall   out of the ordinary, strange

ON

On a shoestring   with little money to spend, tight budget

On board   (actively) involved

On sale   selling for a special low price

On schedule   as planned (in terms of time)

On target   according to schedule

On the ball   (to) be prepared, in good shape

On the brink   almost, almost ready, on the edge, on the verge

On the fly   fast, spontaneously

On the line in danger of being lost, at stake *[my job is on the line]*

On the mark standard, appropriate

On the minus side disadvantages, drawbacks, (*syn*) snags

On the plus side advantages, benefits

On the way almost ready, in process, in production

(to be) **on top of** (to) be in control, follow, not lose sight of

One-size-fits-all for every situation, universal

One-stop-shopping multi-product, multi-service

One up one step ahead

Onetime former

Onset/outset beginning, start

Open mind: (to have an ~) (to) not judge without understanding

Opportunity chance, possibility

Organizational culture the way things are expected to be done in an organization

Out: ((a) week ~) later *[task yourself a week out to check it]*

(to be) **out in left field** (to) be completely uninformed about what is going on

Out of character not typical (behavior of a person)

Out of (smb.'s) league not at somebody's level, overqualified, superior

Out of line not agreeing with what is right or usual

Out of the loop uninformed; (*ant*) to be in the loop

(to go) **out on a limb** (to) take a risk; in a risky position

Outside the box creative, unusual

Outsource   subcontract, contract out

Outsourcing   using an outside company for a specific task

Over one's head beyond one's ability to understand, not understandable; to a higher manager, more important person

Overhaul   (to) fix, rebuild, repair, transform

Overhead   cost of conducting business (salaries, rent, etc.)

Overkill   (to) over-do, do more than necessary

P

Package container, packet, set

Pan off (to) change the subject, focus away; to give to somebody else

Pan out (to) have a (good) result; to work out in the end

Paradigm the standard (business) model *[business paradigm]*

Part of the equation part of the whole

Pass on (savings) (to) result in low cost *[sales savings are passed on to the customer]*

Pass the buck (to) shift responsibility

Pay through the nose (to) pay too high a price, pay too much

Payout (to) give out money

PC *(acr)* a **p**ersonal **c**omputer

Peace of mind relief from stress, peace, calmness, serenity

Peak (to) reach the highest point

Pension (monthly) payment received after retirement

Pep rally a motivational meeting

Pep talk a motivational speech, so that people do not give up and try harder

Pet peeve something which is bothersome or annoying

Pick out (to) choose, identify, select

Pick (smth.) up and run with it (to) accept a project and do to the best of one's abilities, *(syn)* go with it

Pick up (to) assume responsibility; choose; learn

Pick up the slack (to) do extra work (small projects); tighten up procedures *[Danielle, could you pick up the slack?]*

(A) **piece of cake!** This is easy!

PII *(acr)* **p**ersonal **i**ndividual **i**nformation

Pilot first (test) product, program *[pilot product, program]*

Piss off *(sl)* (to) annoy, bother, make angry

Pitch *(inf)* a talk to persuade somebody to buy or do something; a brief self-introduction presenting yourself favorably; (to) sell *[a sales pitch]*

Pitch in (to) contribute

PLAY

Play by ear (to) improvise, make decisions on the go

Play into (the culture of a company) (to) conform to, relate to

Play out (to) turn out

Play phone tag *(inf)* unsuccessful attempt to make contact (between two persons)

Play with one's schedule (to) rearrange one's day

Players participants, companies

Playing field the market

Plunge (to) fall suddenly, dramatically

Point important issue

Point out (to) bring to attention, indicate

Pointer(s) advice or important issues to follow in a presentation; tool used in a presentation to point to key issues

Position (to) present in a certain way (a product, an idea)

Positive optimistic

Pow wow *(inf)* (to) huddle; short, informal meeting

PR *(acr)* **p**ublic **r**elations

Pragmatist practical person, down-to-earth person, someone concerned with practical values and results

Prize: (keep your eyes on the ~) stay focused {See: **Keep one's eye on the ball**}

Proactive initiating action beforehand to prevent something (negative) from happening

Process business procedures, the way business operates

Procrastinate to put off doing something until a future time or right before a deadline

Product item for consumption, merchandise, final output

Profile (high profile) status in the industry (very important) *[high profile account or client]*

Promise the sun and the moon (to) promise a lot (without delivering the promise), make unrealistic promises

Prompt (to) cause, induce

PULL

Pull (to) extract, get information *[pull the data from the report]*; remove

Pull back (to) reduce, take out

Pull data (to) extract, get data

Pull (smb.'s) leg (to) fool someone

Pull (smb./smth.) out (to) disengage, take out *[we need to pull Ana out of the project]*; decrease momentum

Pull strings (to) influence

Pull the plug (to) end; expose someone's secret or confidential activities

Pull together (to) develop, get organized; unite

Purge (to) eliminate (employees) in leadership position

PUSH

Push: (to be a ~) (to) emphasize, give importance to *[this product is a big push]*

Push ahead (to) make progress

Push back (to) delay, make a lesser priority

Push the envelope ask for too much; get more than deserving, take advantage by wanting more; exceed desired criteria *[you are pushing the envelope when you drive the car faster than it is designed to be driven]*

PUT

Put a positive spin on present favorably; focus on positive

Put all the pieces together (to) carefully combine resources, put certain steps into place in order to achieve a goal

Put (smb.) in a bad spot (to) make vulnerable *[she really put us in a bad spot]*

Put onto a radar screen (to) add to the situation, take notice; make something worth notice; keep in mind

Put one's mind to it (to) analyze, study in great detail; focus intensely

Put stock into believe *[don't put any stock into what she says, she has a history of lying]*

Put the breaks on (to) discontinue, slow, stop

Put the cart ahead of the horse (to) switch the expected procedure around; put Step B before Step A, put something in a reverse order

Put two and two together (to) deduce based on facts

Q

Q&A *(acr)* **Q**uestions and **A**nswers

Quick fix   fast solution

Quit   *(inf)* (to) leave a job on one's own will (may have a negative connotation), *(syn)* leave a job

R

Radar: (on the ~) under attention, observation

Raise a flag (to) caution, warn

Raise a stink *(vulg)* (to) protest strongly

Raise the bar (to) increase standards

Ramble (to) be wordy and not get to the point

Ramifications implications, consequences

Range: (long ~) long term *[long- range plans]*

Rapport accord, harmony, understanding

Rat race confusing and chaotic activity without purpose or result (in fast-paced environment) *[sometimes my days at the office feel like a rat race]*

RAW

Raw deal unfair treatment

Read between the lines (to) deduce the unsaid meaning

Record highest ever *[record sales]*

Recycle (to) reprocess *[recycle paper]*, reuse *[recycle an idea]*

Red tape bureaucracy, bureaucratic process

Red flag attention, caution, warning

Reduce (to) decrease, diminish, lessen

Result-driven focused on results and goals

Result in (to) bring about, bring rise to, be occasion of

Retirement permanent end to a career or job

Revenue funds (money) coming into the company as a result of sales

Right off the bat immediately, right away

Right on the nose exact (on time) *[She was given 3 minutes to speak and she finished right on the nose]*, *(syn)* right on the money

Ring a bell (to) remind of something, sound familiar

Rise to the occasion (to) meet the challenge

Robust strong (solution, system)

Rocker: (off one's ~) crazy, far fetched, unrealistic

Rocket (to) rise quickly and dramatically

Rocky difficult, rough, with obstacles

ROLL

Let's **roll** let us start! let us get going, let us do it

Roll out (to) launch (a new product or service)

Roll up one's sleeves (to) get down to work

Rolling along moving along (with a project)

Rookie an inexperienced employee, someone new at something

Roughly approximately

Round robin a collaborative letter or activity passed between several members of a group

Rubbernecking curiosity delay on the road

Rule of thumb basic rule

Rules of engagement rules of conducting business

RUN

Run (smth.) by (smb.) (to) consult with somebody before taking action *[I will write a proposal and run it by you]*

Run into a wall {See: **Hit a wall**}

S

Sales pitch a short presentation or talk aimed at persuading or selling

Save face (to) maintain a good reputation

Save the day (to) bring success when it was almost unattainable

Scoop essence, heart of the matter *[here is the scoop]*, *(syn)* jist

Scramble (to) go around the obstacles; work quickly to finish a project

Screen out (to) exclude by comparing with competition

Screw *(sl)* (to) cheat

Screw (smth.) (up) *(sl)* (to) make an error, a mistake; disappoint, *(syn)* let down

Self-starter a person who takes initiative (at work)

Sell like hotcakes (to) sell as the item is available, almost faster than can be produced

Sell on (concept, idea) (to) accept; persuade

Sell (smb.) short (to) underestimate someone

SET

Set a level of (to) put forth or present a standard model of *[these business tools set a level of good practice that will improve productivity]*

Set-back a delay, disadvantage, failure

Set off (to) cause

Set out (to) decide *[set out to accomplish something]*

Set up (to) establish, start; provide money

Severance payment an employee receives upon leaving a job

Sexual harassment inappropriate (from an American standpoint) behavior when interacting with the opposite sex

Shake out (to) eliminate competitors; fix (glitches in a system)

Shake up unexpected result; (to) initiate action, rearrange *(syn)* mix up

Shakedown test

Shape (to) affect, influence

Shell out (to) spend

Shift gears (to) change the subject *[now I'd like to shift gears and speak about...]*

Shit hit the fan *(vulg)* something went terribly wrong

Shoot for (to) try; plan for

Shoot one's mouth off (to) express one's opinion loudly and rudely; boast

Shoot oneself in the foot (to) harm oneself

Shoot the breeze (to) chat, talk informally

Shortcut shorter and direct path

Shot in the arm something encouraging, inspiring, motivating

Show up (to) appear; attend

Shrink (to) become smaller

Sink money into (to) invest large amounts of money into a project, business

Six Sigma way of measuring processes, a comprehensive system for sustaining business performance, success and leadership

Slam dunk success from perfect timing and positioning

Slap (smth.) on (smth.) (to) apply something very quickly; construct poorly

Slice of the pie part, a percentage

Slug it out (to) hash smth. out, to get down to detail

Slump period of economic inactivity or decline

Small fish unimportant person or thing

Smuggle (to) import or pass through the border illegally

Snag (to) capture, grab, grasp, take; obstacle

Soar (to) rise sharply

Social security retirement income for workers from the US government (usually small)

Soft sell non-aggressive approach to selling

Song: (for a ~) for very little money

Sort out (to) clarify, organize

Soup to nuts everything

Spam advertising e-mail

SPEAK

Speak for itself obvious

Speak to (smth.) (to) explain something

Speak volumes (to) convey a lot of meaning with few words or actions

Spearhead (to) head, lead

Spill the beans (to) reveal a secret

Spin: (to put a ~ on) (to) position

Spin one's wheels work hard but get nowhere

Square away (to) sort out

Square One from the start

Spread oneself too thin (to) try to do too much

STAND

Stand a chance (to) have an opportunity for success, *(ant)* stand no chance, stand a snowball's chance

Stand-alone (device) function separately, independently

Stand as (to) represent

STAR: (Situation **T**ask **A**ction **R**esult**)** interviewing technique based on the premise that a person's recent, relevant past performance is the best indicator of future performance

Starting point beginning

Stats *(abbr)* numerical data, statistics

Status quo normal, as it should be

STAY (AHEAD)

Stay afloat (to) remain in business

Stay ahead of the curve (to) foresee changes; in favorable position

Stay ahead of the game (to) have an advantage, be prepared

Stay on target (to) not get distracted, keep the goal in mind, stay focused, *(syn)* keep an eye on the ball

Steep *(sl)* extreme *[extreme measures]*

Steering committee a group responsible for guiding a project

Stem (from) (to) originate (from)

STEP

Step by step gradually

Step up (to the plate) (to) take a risk, take initiative

Steps to take actions to take

STICK

Stick around (to) not leave, stay

Stick it out (to) keep going, not give up, persevere, *(syn)* hang in there

Stick one's neck out (to) take a risk

Stick to one's guns (to) insist, maintain one's position or opinion, persevere

Stock inventory; (to) have on hand, readily available

Streamline (the processes, work) make more efficient, simplify

Stress anxiety, pressure, strain

Stressed out anxious, strained, stressed, worried

STRETCH

Stretch (to) embellish, exaggerate, lie

Stretch oneself (to) challenge, stimulate

Stretch too thin (to) be involved in too many activities, too busy

Strike out (to) fail to complete, miss an opportunity

Success achievement, accomplishment, triumph, victory

Successful triumphant, victorious, winning

Suck up to flatter for personal gain

Surf (to) visit web sites on the internet

SWEAT

Sweat preoccupy, worry *[do not sweat the small stuff]*

Sweet deal a profitable agreement, arrangement

Synergy added energy

Synopsis abstract, outline, summary

T

TABLE

Table: (on the ~) out in the open, in front of an audience for discussion *[do you feel that we got all the issues on the table?]*

Tailor adjust for a specific person or thing *[tailor a product to the client's needs]*

TAKE

Take point of view, opinion

Take: (what is your ~ on that?) What is your opinion? What is your point of view?

Take a step further (to) do something additional

Take a time out (to) regroup, take a break to reorganize

Take after (to) be like; inherit

Take at face value (to) accept things as they appear

Take away (to) learn; lesson learned (after a presentation or workshop)

Take care of (to) attend to, help *[I will take care of this problem for you]*

Take-charge (employee, manager) a person who uses initiative and authority to take action and accomplish goals

Take it and run with it! make a project your own (responsibility)

Take it away! (to) start, begin, commence, go ahead

Take it to another level (to) increase its importance or value

Take it up a notch (to) increase activity, improve, *(syn)* heat it up

Take off (to) have a good start; become dramatically successful

Take on (a responsibility) (to) be responsible for *[who is going to take on that responsibility?]*

Take out (to) eliminate

Take over (to) take control

Take (smb.) up (on one's offer) (to) accept something that is offered

Take the bait (to) get caught, get trapped

Take the bullet for (smb.) (to) accept fault or responsibility, take somebody else's blame

Take toll (to) affect negatively, damage

Target (to) aim toward a goal, objective *[companies are targeting overhead costs for cuts]*

Targeted under attack

Task assignment, chore, job

Task force a group of people, a committee established to accomplish (a business goal) (usually temporary in nature

TBD *(acr)* **t**o **b**e **d**etermined

Team player a person who relates to and works well with others

TGIF *(col)* **t**hank **G**od **i**t's **F**riday

The whole nine yards everything

Think on one's feet (to) think fast, think spontaneously, without preparation

Think outside the box (to) be creative

Thrive (to) do very well, succeed

Throw a curve ball unexpectedly change the parameters of your work or project, *(syn)* reshuffle the ducks; ask a shocking interview question

Time crunch time limitations, restrictions

Time out (to) rest, take a break

Timeframe time allotted for a job to be completed

Timeline chronological order of events

Tip point, word of advice

To your point adding to what was said

Tongue in cheek (to say something) mockingly or sarcastically

Tool device, instrument

Toot one's own horn (to) boast, self-promote

Top best quality, highest price

Top-brass top level management; the best *(syn)* the cream of the crop

Top gun an influential or powerful person, best performer

Top notch best quality

Top of the line {See: **Top notch**}

Top side general, not detailed

Touch base (to) consult on a particular situation

Tough difficult, challenging

TPM *(acr)* **t**otal **p**erformance **m**anagement

TRACK

Track (mistakes, results) (to) maintain a record of

Track: (on ~, stay on ~) (to) not deviate from the goal

Trade off in exchange for another

Transaction (business) buying or selling; operation or action

Translate into (to) mean, result in

Tread madly (to) work fast and with minimal quality

Trenches the center of job activity

Trigger (to) cause

Turn around (a business) (to) make successful again,

recover *[the economy will turn around]*

Turn around time
time in which service is delivered; how long it takes to complete something

Trip over oneself   (to)
act prematurely; be extremely eager

Trump card   the most valuable resource saved for use in the ultimate hour of a project

Two sides of the coin
advantages and disadvantages, pluses and minuses

Two-way street   both parties should be mindful about something

U

Under a cloud   under unfavorable or negative circumstances

Under duress   under a lot of pressure, under a lot of stress

Underscore   (to) emphasize, highlight

Unit   a section of a company, (the whole) part of a system or device

Up and running operational, started

Up front   beforehand; honest, direct

Up to par   equal to the standard level or usual quality, *(syn)* up to the mark

Up to snuff   up to expected standards

Up to the mark   {See: **Up to par**}

Update   (to) keep informed, keep posted

Upset   (to) annoy, disappoint, displease, offend *[implementing outsourcing often means the loss of some jobs, which can upset employees]*

Upside   advantage, benefit, positive side

Uptake   when a client signs up to buy something

V

Validate (to) confirm, endorse

Value added/ value-add of an increased quality, standard, value

Vision image, mental picture, realistic dream, visualization *[vision for the company's future]*

W

Water down (to) make weaker

Way to go! Good! Excellent Plan!

Wear different hats (to) have different roles, jobs, positions (at the same time)

Wet blanket dull or boring person who ruins fun for others at a party

Wet paint fresh, new, recently done

WFM (*acr*) what's in it for me?

When it comes down to it in essence

Willy-nilly thrown together without prior planning

Win-win mutually beneficial

Wing it (to) do something unprepared or spontaneous (in a negative sense)

Wire: (down to the ~, under the ~) at the very last moment

Wired constructed, configured, put together *[I was not wired that way]*

White paper a study by an expert in the field

Work every angle of an issue (to) analyze and solve a problem from all sides

Work flow a sequence of steps necessary to perform a task; distribution of duties necessary to perform a task

Wrap up (to) finish (a letter, a project)

Write off loss; expense

X

Y

You bet!   indeed, yes

You got it!   Yes! that is correct! that's right!

Z

Zero in on   (to) aim at

Additional List of Expressions

24/7   all day, everyday

80/20 rule   the idea that 80% of business comes from 20% of the customers

360 evaluation   an evaluation that reviews all aspects of an employee

All hands on deck!   everyone ready to work!

All set   ready!

(to not) **have a bandwidth**   there is a breakdown in the flow of data (computer phrase)

It's like drinking from a fire hydrant   overwhelming feeling from the abundance of information on the internet

It is harder than nailing Jell-O to the wall   impossible

It is like herding cats   {See: **It is harder than nailing Jell-O to the wall**}

It is not one's cup of tea   not enjoyable or liked, not a right job for someone

It is not rocket science   it is not complicated, (syn) it is not brain surgery

Keep that positive attitude!   (to) maintain an optimistic view, not be affected by others or one's own negative attitudes

New take on old words fresh   new idea on an old or common situation

Not a happy camper   unhappy person

Put your money where your mouth is   (to) do what one has promised

Right on the money   exactly, precisely

Run it up the flagpole and see who comes barking (to) advertise

Something has gotta give   something bad is most likely to happen and soon

Stick out like a sore thumb   (to) be noticeably different from others

That's about it   that is all

That's (smb.'s) plug   it is somebody's input, contribution, opinion

This is not set in stone   it is not final, it may change or be changed

This is (smb.'s) two cents worth   this is somebody's small piece of advice

To put all eggs in one basket   (to) rely/count on a particular outcome

Walk the walk and talk the talk   (to) do what you say, to follow your own example

Way to go!   Good job! Excellent!

You got it!   Yes, that's right

Take Control of Your Own Vocabulary

Your ability to achieve success depends on your ability to communicate effectively. Taking control of your vocabulary is a huge part of it. If you improve your vocabulary you will create the impression of a confident professional. You will also improve your business and social confidence. Confidence and professionalism will help you become more competitive and successful.

Building a powerful vocabulary is not as difficult as you might think. Remember that a relatively small number of words and phrases makes up the majority of what we say.

- **Know what words to learn**. Knowing what words to learn is the first step to acquiring effective vocabulary.
- **Make a list of subjects and typical situations** that you encounter every day in your life and work. Using the worksheet below, create your own glossary of those words. *First do it alphabetically. Then group by subject or situation.*
- **Read.** Read as much as you can. I really like detective thrillers by modern American writers. They reflect modern American spoken language with idioms and Americanisms in abundance. Do not look up every unknown word in the dictionary. Take notice of ones that you come across over and over again.

Look them up, translate and make them part of your
active vocabulary.
- **Listen.** Listen to books on tape by modern American
  writers. Take notice of the words and expressions
  that occur over and over again. Capture them and
  make a part of your vocabulary. This can serve double
  duty, you will also improve your listening skills and
  will help to reduce your accent.
- **Use.** As you replenish your vocabulary, try to use new
  words and expressions when you speak or write.

To maximize your study time and accelerate memorization,
capture and study the essential vocabulary words for your
field. When selecting the words and expressions for
improving your vocabulary, keep in mind three word
categories.
  1. Category I. Units of general use. Examples: *I, go,
     please, yes, no.*
  2. Category II. Units common to all businesses.
     Examples: *analyze, money, report.*
  3. Category III. Units vital to your profession (lingo,
buzzwords, terms). Examples for hospitality industry:
booking, room rate, check in, check out.

Using the template below, create a list of words and
expressions you frequently encounter in your work.
Memorize them and use them daily.

My Ameri$peak

YOUR NAME

Category I
Words and Phrases of General Meaning

Word or Phrase	Definition/Translation
A piece of cake!	*This is easy!*
Speak	
Go	
Immediately	

Category II
Words or Phrases Essential to All Businesses

Word or Phrase	Definition/Translation
Flow chart	a diagram showing steps of a business process
Pep rally	a motivational meeting
Pick up	choose; learn

Category III
Terms Specific to My Profession
(Below are hospitality industry examples)

Word or Phrase   **Definition/Translation**

Booking rate

Check in

Check out

Accent Reduction

What is an accent? Simply put, an accent is the combination of pronunciation and intonation. Varying degrees of these two factors result in a variety of different accents.

Pronunciation is the result of such factors as the positioning of the vocal cords, tongue and lips as well as the amount of stress and the duration of sounds while speaking a language. Intonation is the melody, rhythm, and speed of speech. Different languages have different sets of sounds and different melodies of the speech. They also vary by average speed.

When you speak English, your accent depends on your base language. If your base language is lacking some sounds that the English language has, you might have particular difficulty pronouncing those sounds. For example, it may be challenging for native speakers of Russian to pronounce the [H] sound. Native speakers of Spanish and Arabic may have difficulty in pronouncing the sound for [V]. As a rule they would pronounce [B] instead. By the same token, Koreans would pronounce [L] instead of [R], since the [R] sound is non-existent in Korean.

Be proud of your heritage and your accent but, at the same time, be aware that an accent can impact your ability to communicate and, consequently, affect your ability to achieve your goals. If your speech cannot be understood by those in a position to hire you, promote you, increase your salary, or become your family or friends, then the doors to opportunity may be closed to you. You may ask, "Is it realistically possible to eliminate my accent?" If you came to the US as an adult, eliminating your accent altogether may be impossible. That's the bad news (as they say in America). But do not despair! The good news is – it is not at all necessary to eliminate an accent altogether. While a heavy accent makes it difficult to understand your speech, a light accent can work to your advantage as long as others understand what you are saying. Let me explain this.

While Americans tend to have difficulty understanding foreigners with heavy accents, a light accent that does not distract from the clarity of speech is often considered charming and, for certain jobs, can even be a desirable quality in a job candidate. For example, an American company that markets products internationally may realize increased sales through a salesperson who can communicate clearly yet still retain his/her native accent. In this case, the accent has a subtle appeal that can work to establish a rapport (or connection) between the company and the client. Therefore, taking steps to reduce, but not necessarily eliminate, your accent can help you in your job quest.

There are several ways to go about reducing your accent. You can purchase or borrow from your local library an audio or video guide aimed at accent reduction. You can hire either a language pathologist or accent reduction coach. Or you can do what I did: work on your accent reduction yourself using the following tips that proved effective for me. Some of the tips will also help to expand your vocabulary.

- **Listen to American speech and try to emulate American accent.** If you are in the US, you have the advantage of immersion into a live language. In addition to watching movies and listening to TV and radio programs, you can engage yourself in live communication with Americans, anywhere and anytime – for example, at your workplace, the supermarket, and even at the Department of Motor Vehicles.

- **Join Toastmasters**. One of the best ways to mix with Americans and improve your speaking in public is to join a Toastmasters Club. You can find a Toastmasters Club in virtually anywhere. Just go to www.toastmasters.org and look for a club close to you. When you visit or join a club, ask the club members to jot down the words in your speech they did not understand. Practice saying these words at home and incorporate them into your speech at the next meeting.

- **Tape your speech.** Analyze the tapes and jot down frequent mistakes you make. Ask for feedback from others. Create a list of most frequently mispronounced words, expressions and constructions. Work on the list daily; read the units over and over again until you get them right.

- **Read aloud every day.** While you read, tape yourself. Listen to the tapes. Repeat words over and over. Remember, minimizing an accent takes practice.

- **Tape real-life conversations.** Create your own list of the most frequent words and expressions. Pronounce them over and over again until you get them right.

- **Buy or borrow from your local library an audio and a printed version of the same book.** Listen to the audio while following the text. Try to repeat sentences and tape yourself.

- **Listen to the media.** Listen to American reporters speak. They speak standard American English.

- **Borrow tapes from the library.** Make this enjoyable. Listen to the kind of tapes you enjoy most. Do it while you are driving, walking, performing home chores. If you enjoy the book, the time will go by fast and you will have a chance to improve your listening skills and vocabulary as well as work on reducing your accent.

- **Speak slowly and enunciate.** Enunciating means pronouncing the sounds very distinctly. Pay special attention to the endings and vowels.
- **Be persistent.** It is a lot of work, but your efforts will be rewarded. Change does not happen overnight, but it does happen if you are positive and persistent. Remember, persistence is one of the underlying values of the American culture!

Some Resources and Literature

American Accent Training. Ann Cook. Barron's. Matrix Press: USA, 2000. www.americanaccent.com

Accent Reduction Made Easy. Penton Overseas. Abridged edition, January 1, 2003

American English Pronunciation: It's No Good Unless You're Understood (Books 1-3), Donna Hope. Cold Wind Press; Bk & Cassett edition, 1999

Vocabulary for Dummies, Laurie E. Rozakis, Ph.D. Hungry Minds, NY, 2002

www.accurateenglish.com – Accurate English, offers American accent training

www.toastmasters.org – A non-profit organization developing public speaking and leadership skills through practice and feedback. Find out about a club in your area either on the Web site or by calling (949) 858-8255. Toastmasters clubs meet in approximately 80 countries worldwide. No matter where you live, work, or travel, you are likely to find a club in your area.

HOW TO GET A JOB IN THE USA

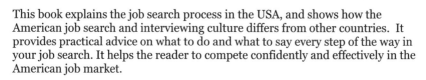

A Step-By-Step Guide to Successful Employment in the United States
(with an Emphasis on American Business *Communication Basics)*

This book explains the job search process in the USA, and shows how the American job search and interviewing culture differs from other countries. It provides practical advice on what to do and what to say every step of the way in your job search. It helps the reader to compete confidently and effectively in the American job market.

You will learn how to:

- Compete in the American job market
- Network and make useful contacts
- Improve your chances of being hired
- Find out about job openings

- Prepare for an interview
- Follow up on an interview
- Negotiate a job offer
- Get the job you want!

And you will learn many communication skills you can apply to life in the USA!

Here's what others are saying:

"The approach in this book and the way information is presented makes it a very important guide for non-American-born citizens, foreign nationals, and anyone entering or re-entering the American job market. Dr. Venditti is providing a great service by writing *How to Get a Job in the USA* and helping this category of job applicant become a productive part of the workforce in this country." **-Robert K. Lenz, Director, Human Resources and Administration (retired) Fuji Photo Film, USA, Inc.**

"When I read excerpts from this book, the positive influence was so powerful. It inspired me to stop sitting at home and put my resume together. I decided that it was time for me to get out of my old robe and try to do something for myself. Thanks a lot for that piece of your book. When will it be published?" **-Margarita Shiffman, a marketing professional from Russia and a naturalized U.S. citizen**

"This book will be a great help on your way to finding the perfect job! Not only will it help you take your first steps correctly, but it will also help you to understand American culture and how things are done here. It might be useful even if you have always lived here. I would like to have a copy as soon as the book is published." **-David Ponce, Financial Analyst, IBM, Mexican national**

"You brought to my attention ways to expand my contacts and look for opportunities where I never thought to look before. You gave me ideas of how to move ahead in my life." **-Debbie Finkenstein, a job seeker born in the US**

" ...your presentation [based on this book] served as a key vehicle in helping students become creative in identifying and maximizing potential sources of employment. You have an important message to deliver and a manner of delivery that creates a comfortable atmosphere.**-LouAnn Bloomer, President and CEO, TBICO (The Bridge to Independence and Career Opportunities)**

This book is available from your local bookseller, online supplier,
www.SucceedinAmerica.com or by using the order form on the last page

About The Author

recognized by the State of Connecticut as a naturalized US citizen who made contributions to better the lives of refugees and immigrants in this country.

Over the past 25 years she held positions ranging from an educator to in-house international assignment consultant.

Author of 61 published works, she is a third-generation educator and the recipient of a State of Connecticut official citation for her tireless dedication to making a difference in the community.

Dr. Nara Venditti is the president and founder of *Succeed in America!*, a consulting firm that helps individuals and organizations with such issues as workplace-based English language skills, career counseling, employability, customer service, cultural understanding, relocating spouse adjustment and employment. Dr. Venditti is

Throughout her 25-year career, she has been working with adult learners in both academic and business environments. Dr. Venditti is an adjunct lecturer at Western Connecticut State University, columnist in ethnic and business periodicals and a host of Channel 23's Community Forum Public Television Program.

Succeed in America!, LLC
offers customized workshops for your organization.
Here is what the participants are saying:

"(Nara's) sense of humor is nicely integrated into her speeches... it drives home points and keeps the audience involved and listening."
Association For Service Management International Convention, Seminar Participant, Reno, Nevada, USA

E-mail nv@SucceedinAmerica.com or Call (203) 733-6068 or (203) 791-11
www.SucceedinAmerica.com
See workshop descriptions and more testimonials on the next page.

Succeed in America!™
Seminars and Resources for Individuals and Organizations

"One of the powerful parts of the seminar was to be able to connect with a total stranger in just three minutes..."
Trevor King

I had read and studied some parts of your CD and presentation before the interview, was well prepared ...and I got the job!"
Gabriel Gavier

First I thank God and I also thank you for everything you taught us that day" Norma Santos

Succeed in America workshops will help you with:

Workplace-Based English Language Skills
- Provide programs specifically designed for your organization's needs
- Teach your non-native speakers to become confident and effective communicators
- Increase productivity and effectiveness in the workplace
- Build synergy in multicultural and multilingual teams

Employability
- Learn the job search process in the USA
- Learn how to market yourself to American employers
- Find fulfilling employment
- Learn the building blocks of effective communication

American Business Communication 101
- Learn the building blocks of effective communication in business
- Gain confidence and increase your competitiveness
- Enhance your value in the workplace and socially
- Become an effective communicator and get promoted

Global Customer Service
- Listen, speak and communicate over the phone and face-to-face
- Be enthusiastic about your business
- Diffuse tense situations and turn negatives into positives
- Build relationships in the USA and globally

Add these workshops to your training.
E-mail nv@SucceedinAmerica.com or
Call (203) 733-6068 or (203) 791-1107

ORDER FORM

Title	Price	Qty	Total
HOW TO GET A JOB IN THE USA™	$19.99	_____	_____
A Step-By-Step Guide to Successful Employment in the United States (with Emphasis on American Business Communication Basics)			
Ameri$peak™	$14.99	_____	_____
A mini-dictionary of the most common words and phrases you need to know to communicate effectively in American business.			
Multilingual thank-you cards	$9.99	_____	_____
(ten cards per pack)			

Subtotal $_____

Sales tax: Connecticut residents add 6% sales tax $_____
Shipping and Handling: $4 **per book** within USA $_____
$7 **per book** outside USA $_____
Canadian orders must include payment in USD, plus 7% GST $_____

TOTAL $_____

Non-US orders must be paid in US funds. Allow at least 2-3 weeks for delivery. **Quantity discounts are available.**

Name_____

Organization_____

Address_____

City/State/Country _____

Phone_____E-mail_____Fax_____

Please contact us at nv@succeedinamerica.com or
Call (203) 733-6068 or **(203) 791-1107**

Please make your check payable and return to: **Succeed in America, LLC**
PO Box 4724, Danbury, CT 06813-4724, USA
You may pay by credit card online at www.SucceedinAmerica.com